The Walk of a
THOUSAND
Moods

A book by RL Lane

Dedicated to all those who think like me.

"THINK think link a wink

THINK think

Sink rink kink fink mink pink tink...stink." RL Lane

Sink? Is something sinking?

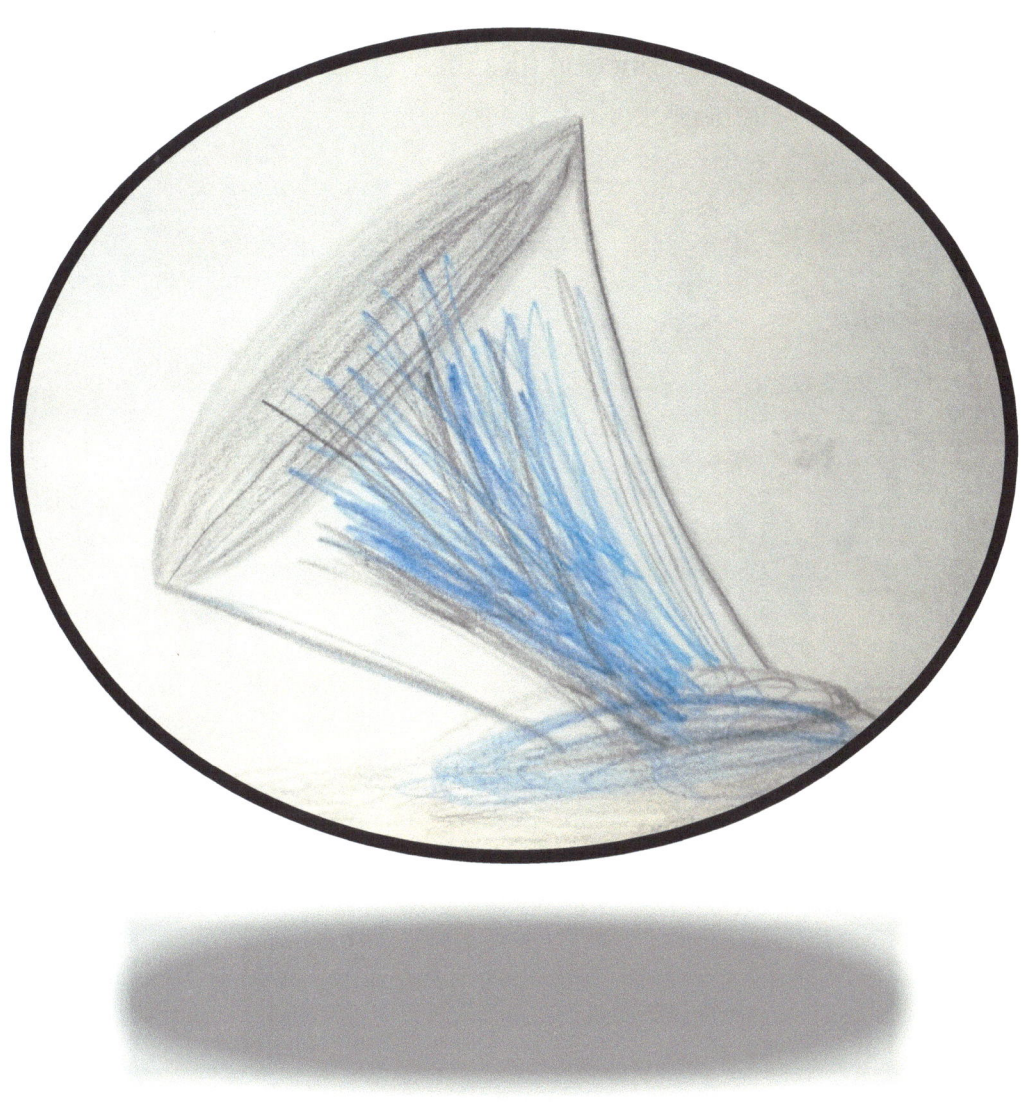

A Time capsule?

By the time I got to the end of the path that day all thousand moods had crossed my mind. From sad to happy to mad to depressed to… "How can a person function like this?" I asked myself. "Does anybody else have this problem?" I ask.

The people passing me on my walk would have seen a different face depending on which mood was crossing my mind at that particular time…

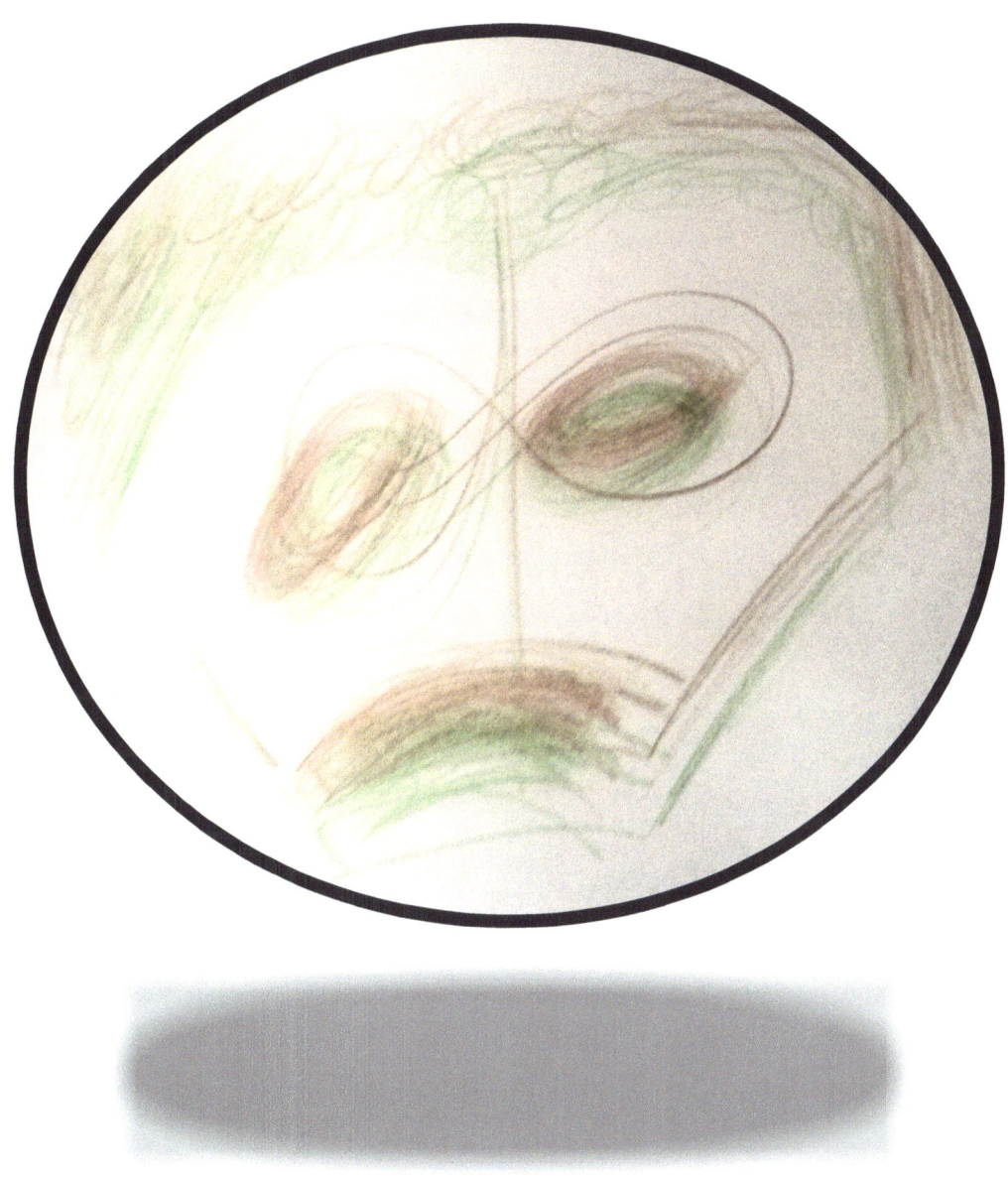

I had passed a deer. He looked hungry. I stopped to fish out the apple in my bag. *Do deer like apples?* He ran away before I could get it out…

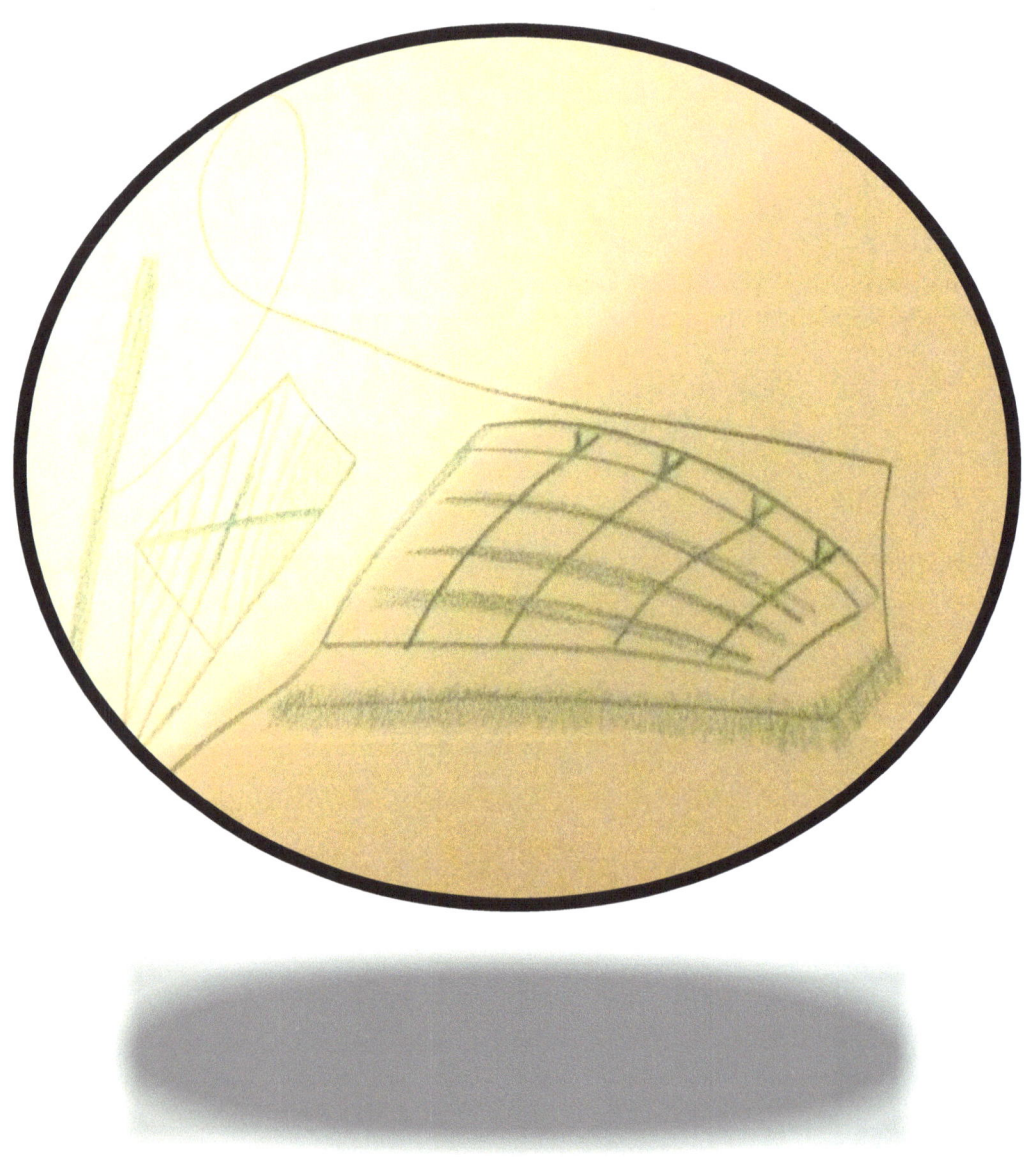

I haven't actually drawn a deer yet. I don't think. This is most likely a horse head…

I did cross a few men. One was tall and cute. He acknowledged my existence. "Was he my soul mate?" I wondered…

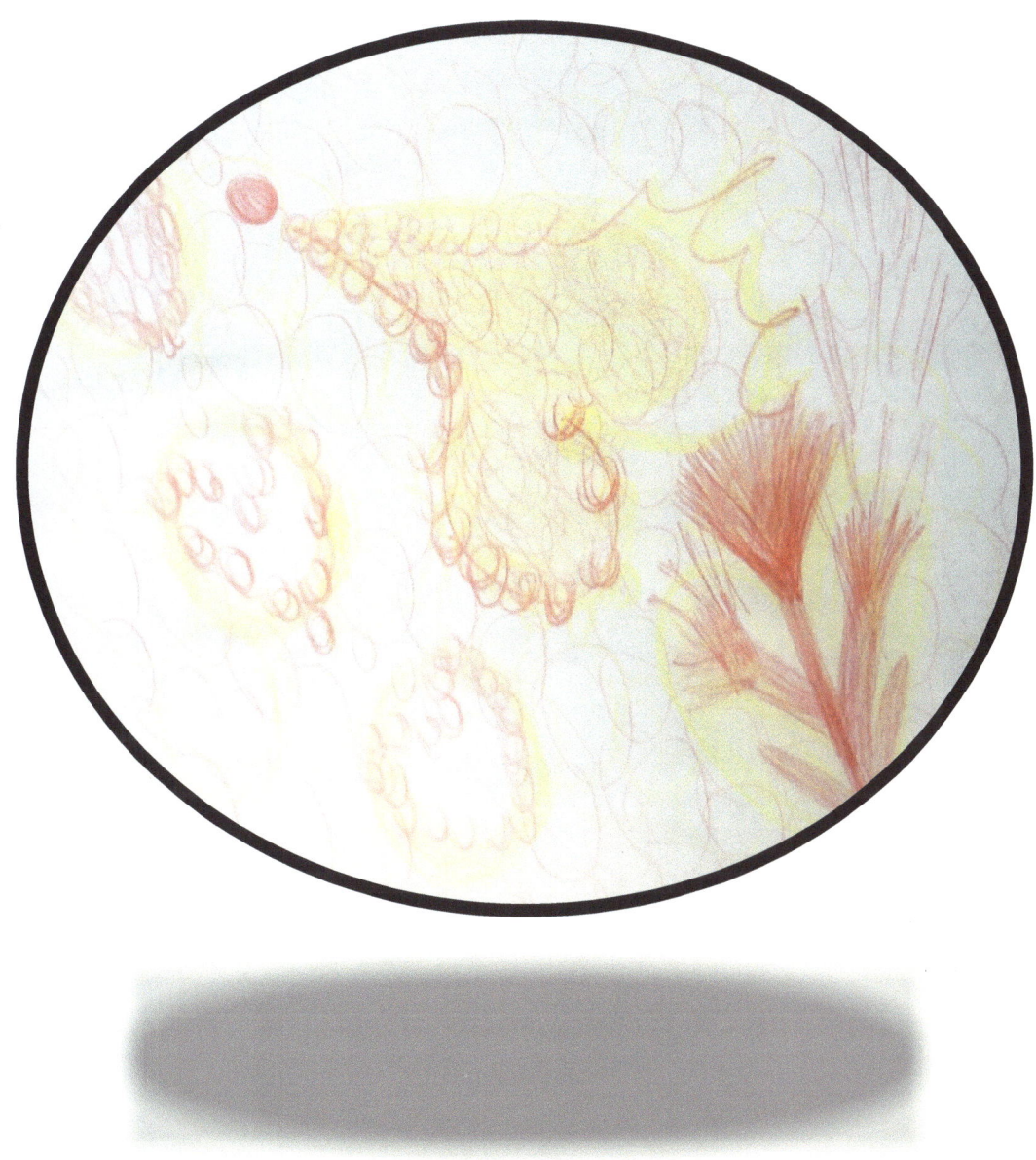

It is probably good that no one can actually see inside my mind. I joked all through EcarreT that the people might be coming for me with the straightjacket, but there were times that I had to at least wonder…

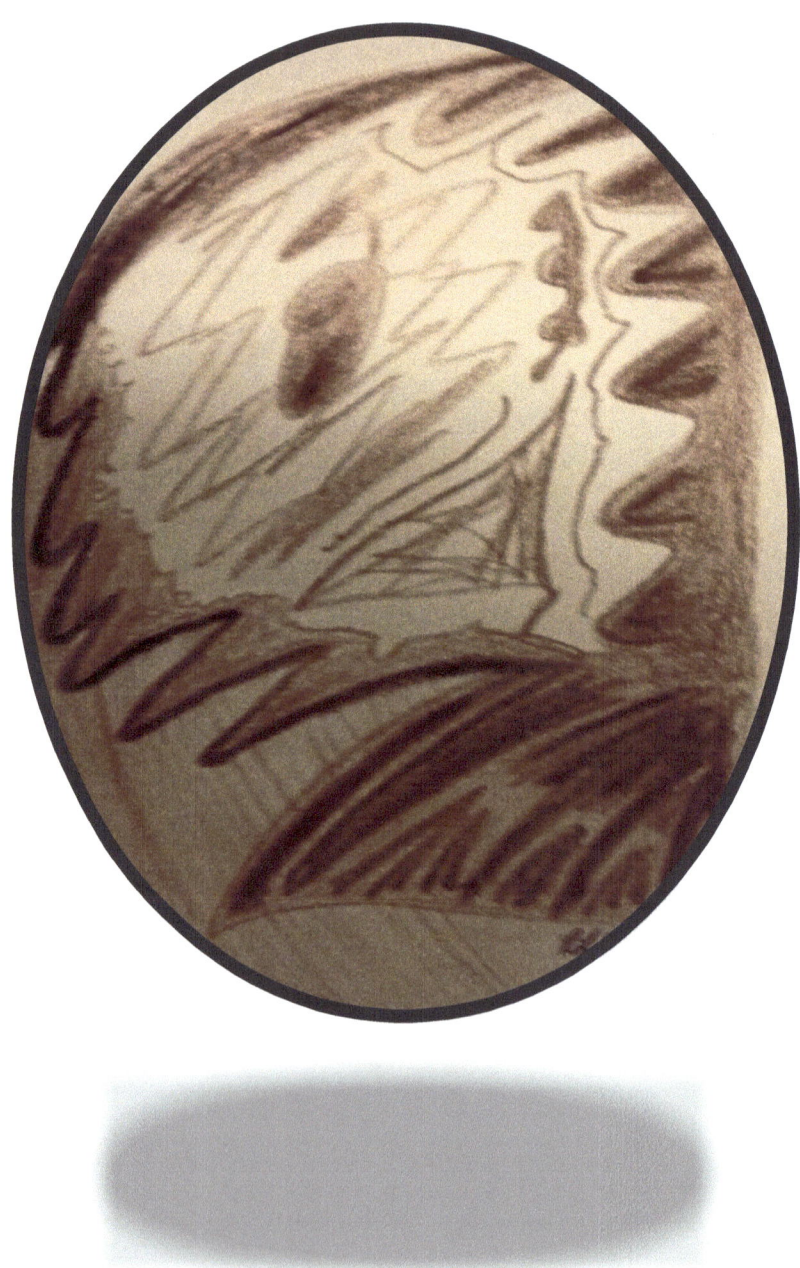

The path I was walking on ran through the woods. I passed a thousand trees. One tree for each mood. By the time I got to the end I had no mood left. Devoid of mood. I felt nothing. It was a welcome feeling considering the array of emotions that had crossed my mind in probably less than an hour…

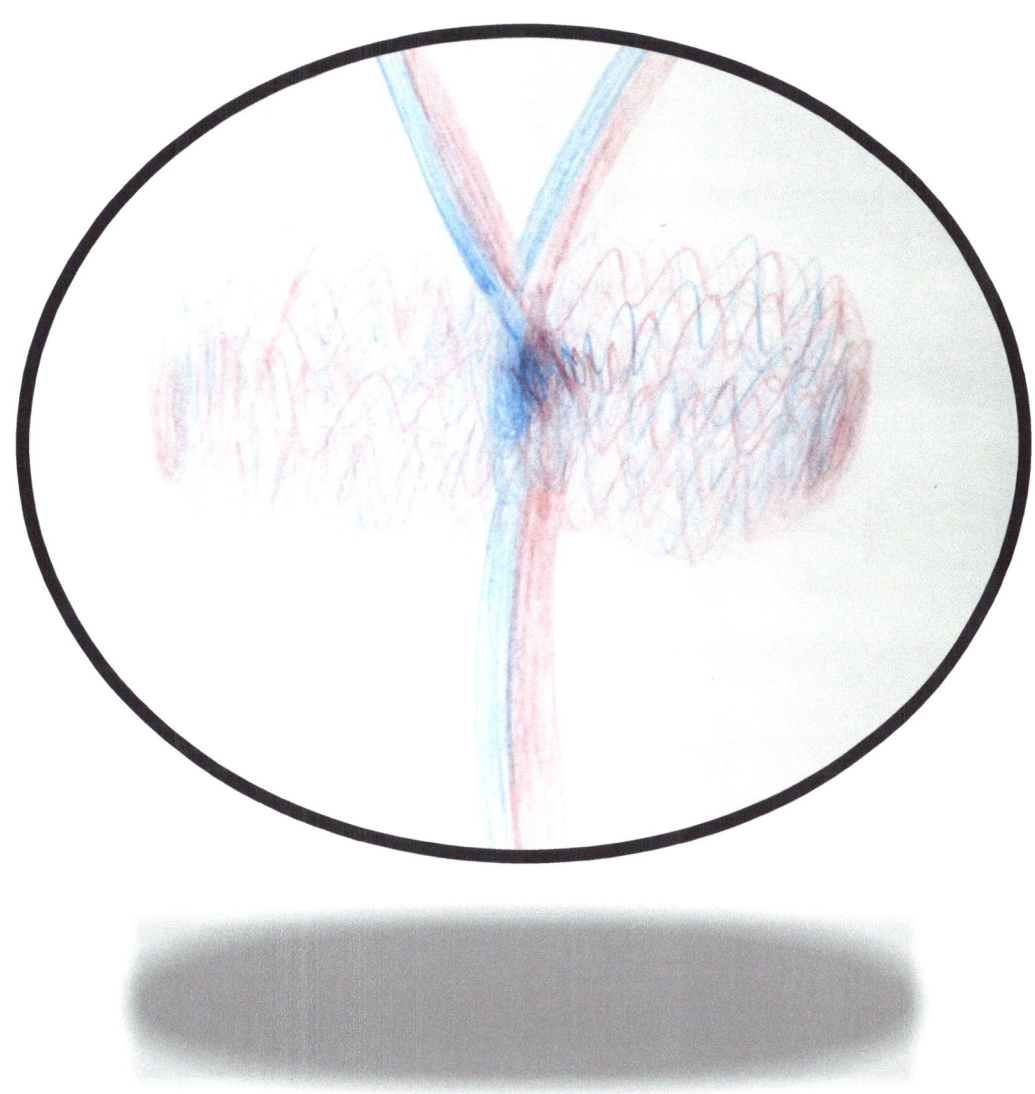

Bitterflies...Butterfleis...Butterflies. I don't remember seeing any butterflies. Oh. Bitter. Yes that mood crossed my mind too.

Fleis? Fleas? I do not like fleas.

I do not want fleas

that is for sure.

I might have this issue

with how my mind works.

I might have this issue

with my mix of emotions.

But at least I do not have

a head full of fleas.

Oh wait! I did see some butterflies!

I had to write about it. To see if there are others with the same problem. You can let me know. My contact information is at the end of the book…

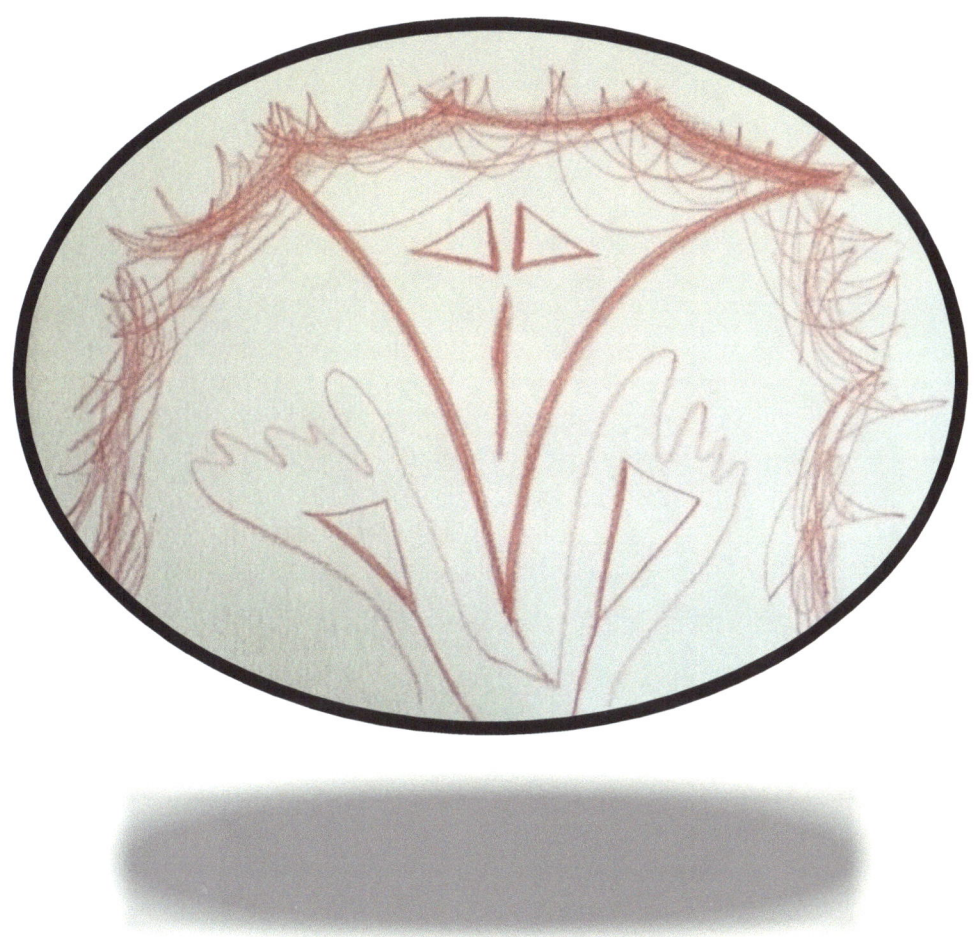

How can anyone expect to make the right decisions in life, if their mood changes with the breeze? I must find a way to not sneeze. *Well, I don't really need to do that, but it rhymed, so I left it there...*

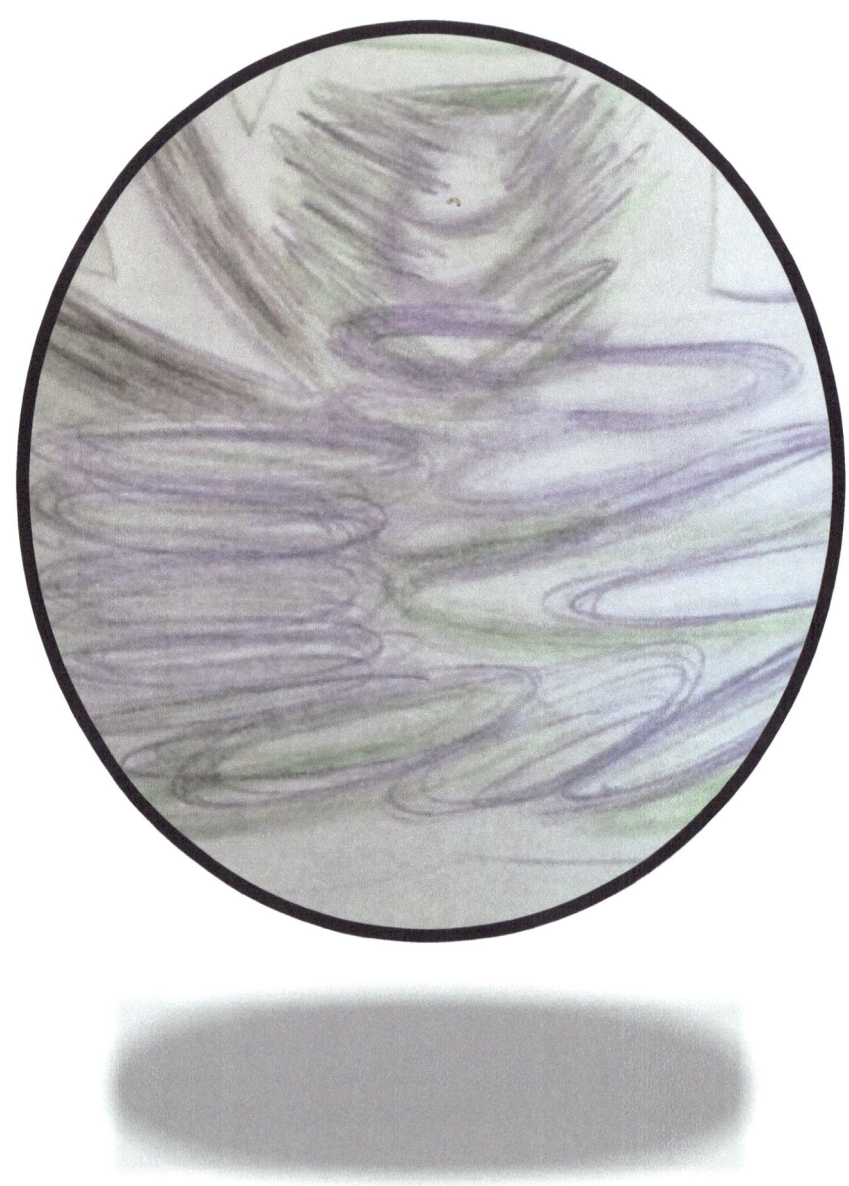

I think sneezes are important. Something about clearing our nasal passages from foreign objects…which reminds me…I found a piece of wood in my bagel this morning. I think it got baked right in the bagel. I took it out and inspected it and then I finished my bagel…

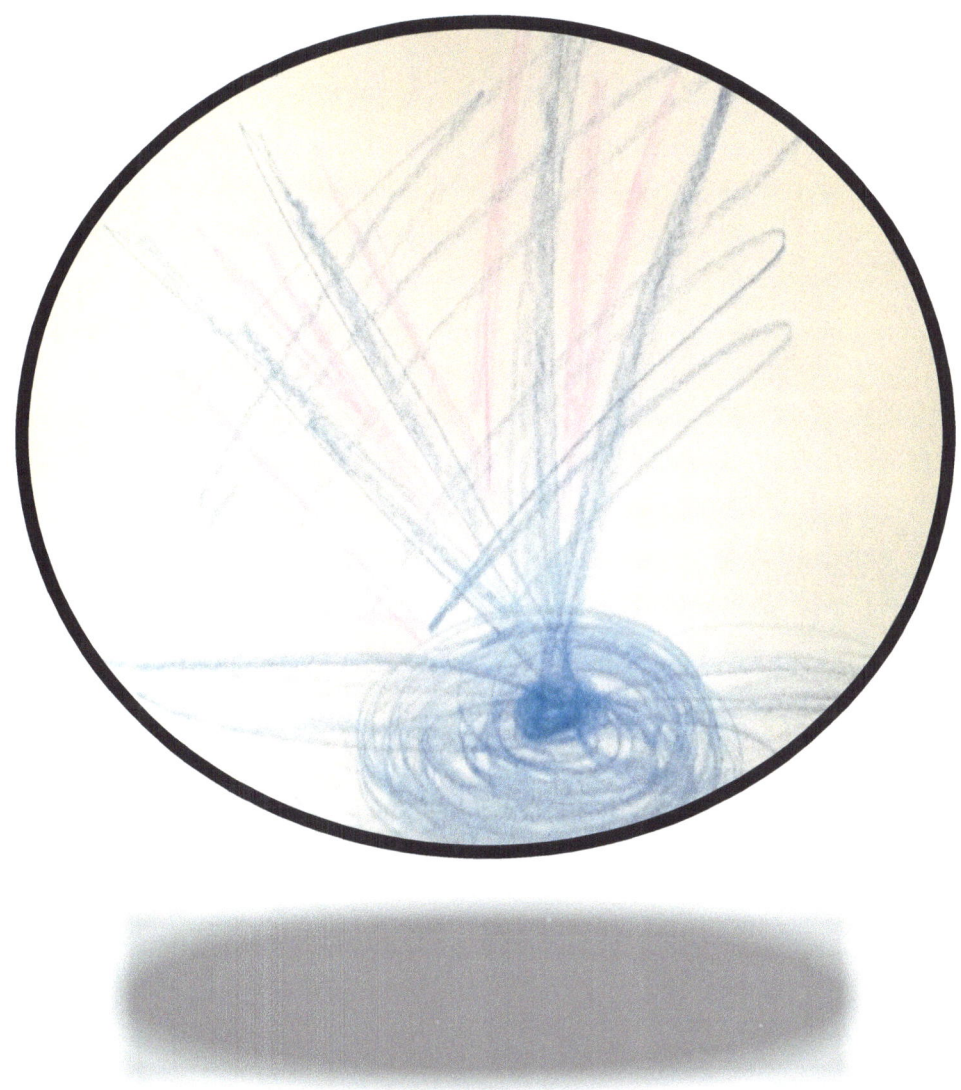

The bagel baker must not have seen that piece of weed…wood. I hope there were no weeds in my bagel. There is not much attention to detail these days. Look at me…I write my books with typos all the time. I tell people they are part of the story…

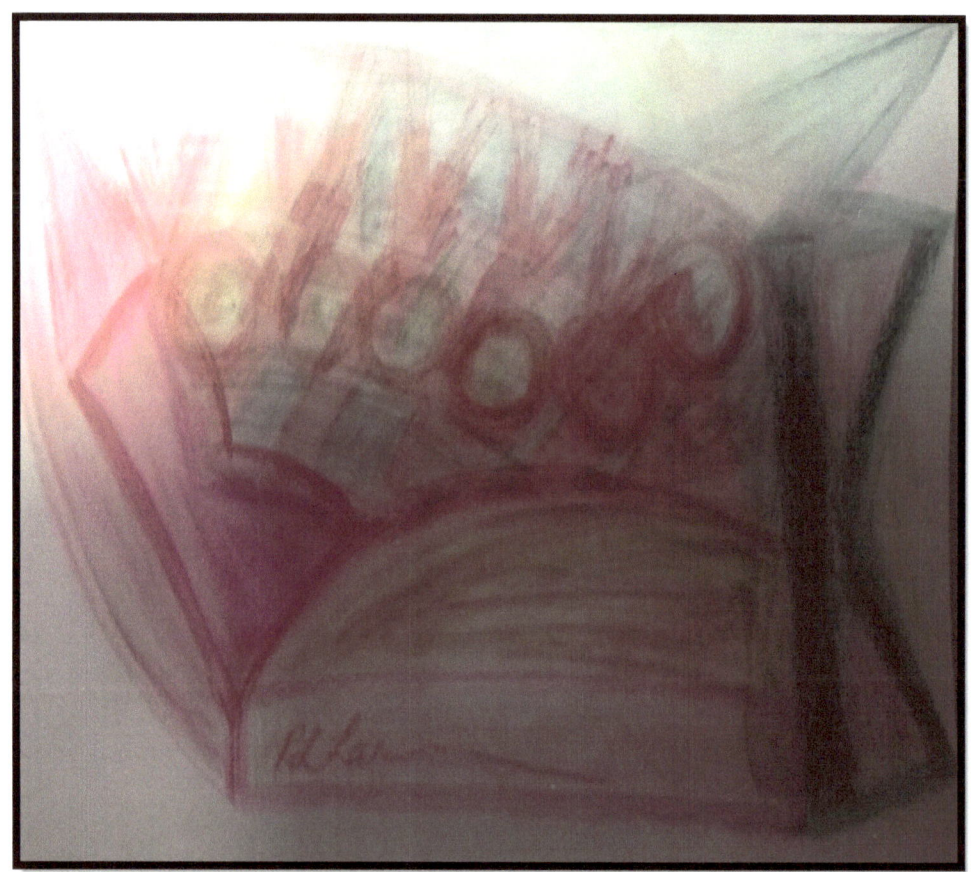

I saw Bob last night. It took me a minute to realize who I was seeing partially because I couldn't believe he would be stopping by. He looked like he did toward the end of his life. He was wearing a baseball cap. I looked him up online and found the recent article about his alleged affairs through the years. I saw a picture of him and his wife in their early years and then another one in their later years.

Oh Mr. Hope. What are we going to say? What do you want me to say? You loved your wife. I know you loved your wife. You loved your family. I know you loved your family. Anyone who knew you would agree…

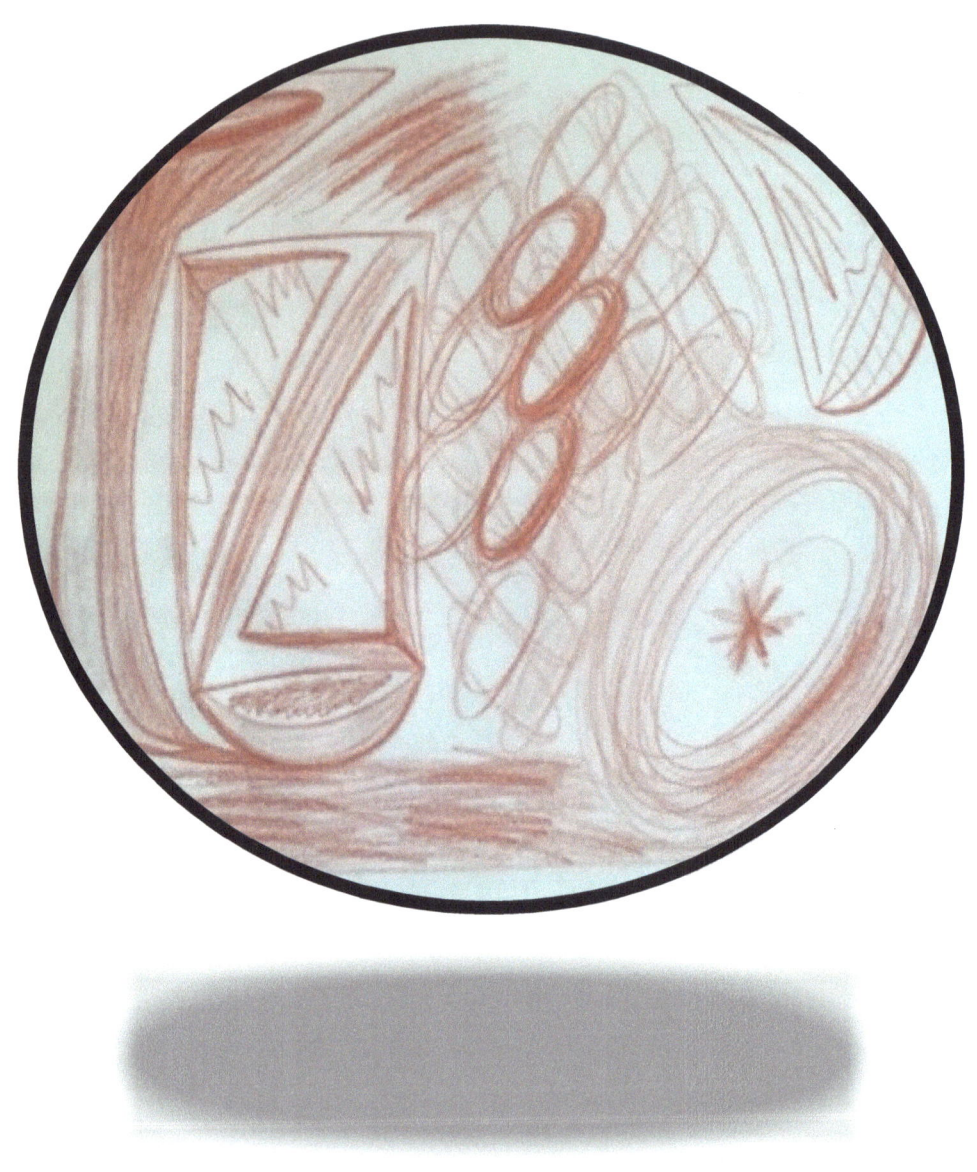

LOVE. Do you see all the letters of love? I see golf balls and the putter. Did Bob love golf too?

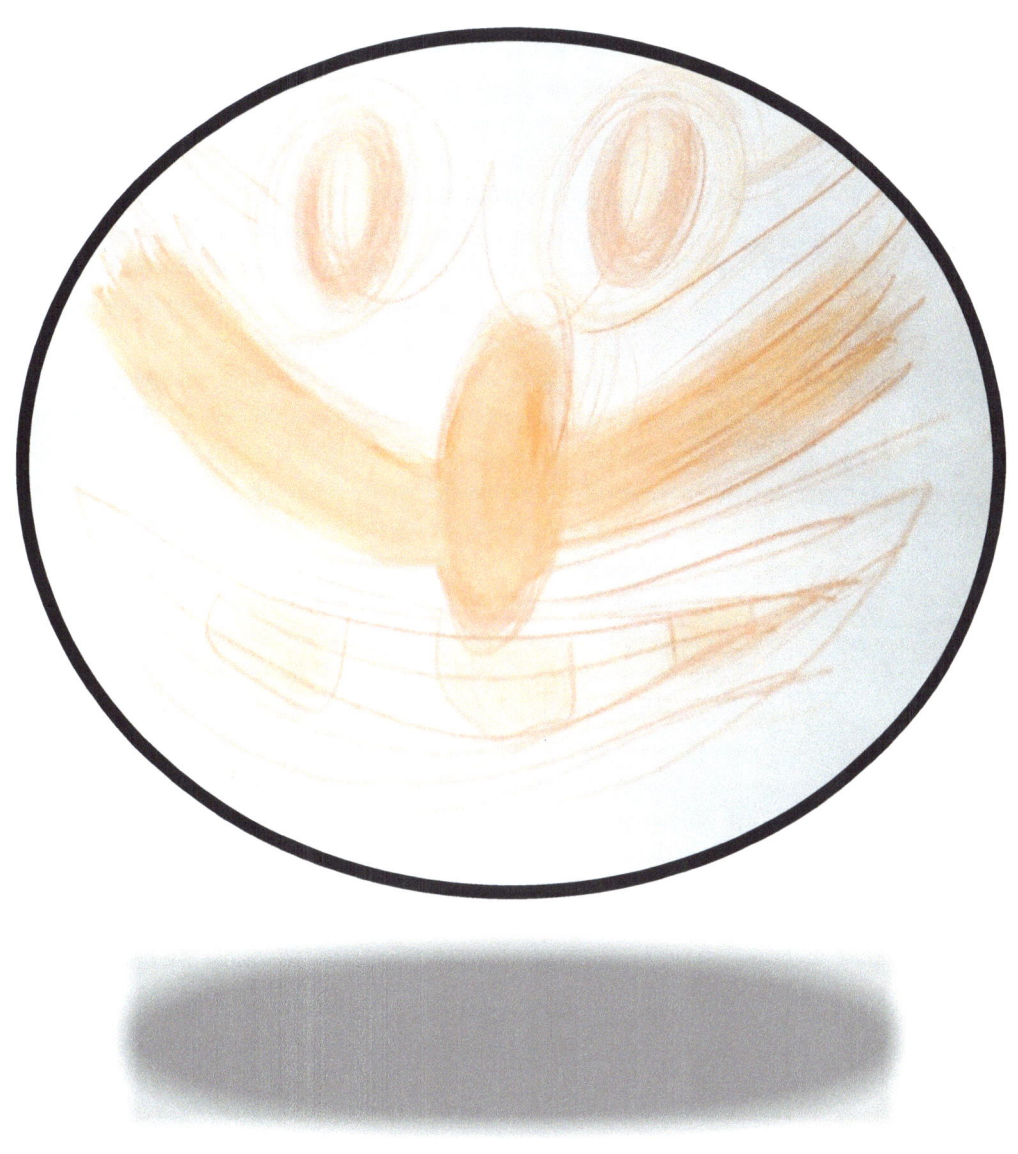

*"Whiskers". Did someone in the family have a cat named Whiskers?
Was it an orange cat?*

The body. They said something to me recently about getting to a point where I didn't have a one-track mind. I have a one-track mind a lot of the time. I get stuck in my one track a lot of time. I keep trying to remember that. ..

Get out of my one track.

Something bigger.

Something bigger.

There is something more for me here than just pleasing my body…

I think that was his message. I Hope I got it right.

I drew four pictures earlier today. I wonder if they belong to this book. Oh. They do. They are the ones you have already seen. People ask me what comes first…the picture or the story. Sometimes the picture. Sometimes the story. Many times I don't even know what all the things are within my own pictures. Sadly, many times I do not even know all the messages within my own books…

My job is to write and draw…it is all I have time for…

Your job is to interpret them…

About the Author and *Illustrator*

RL Lane has published the EcarreT series and a collection of art books featuring the illustrations throughout the books. The series begins with "Chapel Street Signs"…

...unexplained connections that challenge us to beli ve. A woman, a Dad a Doctor, a cat and mouse, a horse and tale tell their stories. "Do you beli ve in spirits?" I asked my friend. "Well look", he said, "I believe there are things that cannot be explained..." Oh. Plus, hear ov a Mom's battle with her struggle to connect to the woman...her little girl.

Welcome to EcarreT...a world
Where everyone cares
Why did I have to create it in...

A fiction fantasy world?

You may already know why, but you will see regardless of what you believe as a girl's journey of love and faith on her "Touring Machine" take her on the best journey of her mundane life. A life well on its way takes a turn in a direction that could've never been seen or even dreamed...

The author can be contacted at:

RosaLeeeLane@gmail.com
www.Amazon.com/author/readrllane

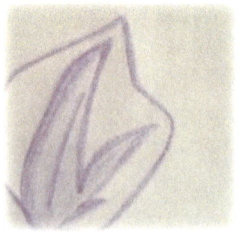

www.ingramcontent.com/pod-product-compliance
Lightning Source LLC
Chambersburg PA
CBHW050433180526
45159CB00006B/2520